D0425745

Becoming a
WELCOMING
CHURCH

OTHER BOOKS BY THOM S. RAINER

We Want You Here
Who Moved My Pulpit?
I Will
Autopsy of a Deceased Church
I Am a Church Member
*Transformational Church**
*Simple Life**
*Essential Church**
*Vibrant Church**
*Raising Dad**
*Simple Church**
The Unexpected Journey
Breakout Churches
The Unchurched Next Door
Surprising Insights from the Unchurched
Eating the Elephant (revised edition)+
High Expectations
The EveryChurch Guide to Growth+
The Bridger Generation
Effective Evangelistic Churches
The Church Growth Encyclopedia +
*Experiencing Personal Revival**
Giant Awakenings
*Biblical Standards for Evangelists**
Eating the Elephant
The Book of Church Growth
Evangelism in the Twenty-First Century+

*Coauthor
+Editor

THOM S. RAINER

NASHVILLE, TENNESSEE

Printed in the United States of America

978-1-4627-6545-4

Published by B&H Publishing Group
Nashville, Tennessee

Dewey Decimal Classification: 254.5
Subject Heading: CHURCH \ CHURCH
FELLOWSHIP \ FRIENDSHIP

1 2 3 4 5 6 7 • 22 21 20 19 18

To

Nellie Jo

Beauty. Compassion. Creativity. Love.

Forty Years of Marriage

Blessing

CONTENTS

ACKNOWLEDGMENTS

If my count is correct, this book is number twenty-seven. I used to think no one read this little section on acknowledgments in my prior books, but I was wrong. I have been amazed to hear from readers who really want to know more about those who influence me, support me, and love me.

You see, this is the part where I give credit where credit is due. These few words are the behind-the-scenes reality of how such a book comes together. This section is not only a reminder, but an acknowledgment of the work and influence of others.

Thank you, B&H team. I am totally amazed how far we have traveled together. I am totally blown away to see how you have become the premier Christian publisher in the world. Thank you to all the B&H team, with specific nods to the leadership of Jennifer Lyell and Devin Maddox.

No work comes from my voice or keyboard without Team Rainer. Many of you have come to know them from the podcasts and the ThomRainer.com blog. You remember their names: Amy Jordan, Amy Thompson, and Jonathan Howe. They are the Nashville team. But over the past year, we have added two virtual team members: Jana Biesecker and Julie Masson. I mean it. I could do no effective work without this team.

I am blessed to be a part of the ministry and organization called LifeWay. I obviously can't name all five thousand employees, but I should. They deserve it. For now, let me give thanks for the leadership and friendship of LifeWay's executive leadership team: Brad Waggoner, Selma Wilson, Eric Geiger, Tim Hill, and Joe Walker. You are all incredible leaders. I can never thank you adequately for all that you do for the Kingdom, for LifeWay, and for me.

One of the greatest joys in my life and ministry is the community of readers, listeners, and subscribers to the various aspects of my platform ministry. I am so grateful for all of you, whether our contact is my books, my blog, ThomRainer.com, my podcasts, Rainer on Leadership and Revitalize and Replant, or my subscription ministry, Church Answers. You have come to learn from me, but I have learned so much more from you.

ACKNOWLEDGMENTS

Of course, you fully expect me to acknowledge my family. If you know anything about me, you know how much I love my family. As I write these words, I am getting ready to leave for a fortieth anniversary trip with my wife and love, Nellie Jo. Please read the dedication page. She deserves it and so much more.

I love and thank God for my three sons and their wives: Sam and Erin, Art and Sarah, and Jess and Rachel. But I am *really* thankful for the ten Rainer grandchildren they have given Nellie Jo and me: Canon, Maggie, Nathaniel, Will, Harper, Bren, Joshua, Collins, Joel, and James.

There are a lot of quotes and interview responses in this book. The names have been changed, and some of the details are different to protect the anonymity of those who were so gracious to speak with me. But all of the events are true.

Now to you the readers of this book: thank you. I do not take for granted you are reading one of my books for the first time or the twenty-seventh time. It is my prayer that this book will be used in your churches for gospel transformation. It is my prayer it will make a difference for the glory of God.

Indeed, it is my prayer that your church will truly become a welcoming church.

CHAPTER 1

Do you have one of those moments in your life when you realized you were not as cool, good-looking, friendly, or smart as you thought you were? I do.

I was a college freshman, dealing with two strong emotions. On the one hand, I loved my new state of independence. On the other hand, I hated my new state of independence. And those aren't contradictory statements.

I thought it was so cool to determine my own schedule, to go where I wanted to go, and do what I wanted to do. Mom and Dad were out of my daily life.

But I missed the relationships, the security, and comfort of home. I was in a new place trying to be independent, trying to figure out what to do next, and trying to make new friends.

It was that latter category where I had a wake-up call: making new friends. You see, I thought Mark and I hit it off well. We seemed to enjoy each other's company. We laughed at one another, and even helped each other with our freshman classes.

So I was particularly pleased when I overheard Mark talking to his parents on the phone. He talked about how much he liked me, how we had become great friends right away, and how I was such a cool guy.

I know. I should not have been eavesdropping. But I enjoyed hearing what a great guy I was so much.

Then he said something that did not make sense. He told his parents where my home was. But it was not my home. It was not even the same state.

It hit me. Mark was talking about someone else with my same first name. His new best friend was Tom, not Thom. I was not the funny and fun guy. I was not the cool guy. I was not his new best friend.

I was devastated.

Wake-up calls can stink. Reality can hurt.

Many churches need wake-up calls. I know. I have worked with hundreds of them on site, and thousands via phone, e-mail, and videoconferences. Many church leaders and members think their churches are healthier than they really are.

Many leaders and members think their churches have better ministries than they really do. And many leaders think their churches are friendlier than they really are.

Before you read further, may I ask you a few questions? Are you willing to set aside your preconceived notions about your church? Are you willing to look at your church more honestly and more clearly? Are you willing to do what it takes to be a welcoming, gospel-centered church?

If not, please close this book, and move onto something else. Don't waste your time here. This book is for those who are willing "to look in the mirror." This book is for those who are willing to face reality. This book is for those who are tired of the same, tame, and lame church life represented by too many congregations.

The Bible has many verses on hospitality. For example, Paul wrote to the church at Rome and to Timothy and Titus about the matter. To the church at Rome, he simply said, ". . . pursue hospitality" (Rom. 12:13). And Paul told Timothy that leaders in the church must be hospitable: "An overseer, therefore, must be above reproach, the husband of one wife, self-controlled, sensible, respectable, *hospitable,* able to teach, not an excessive drinker, not a bully but gentle, not quarrelsome, not greedy" (1 Tim. 3:2–3, emphasis added).

And Paul would say similar words in Titus 1:7–8: "As an overseer of God's household, he must be blameless: not arrogant, not hot-tempered, not an excessive drinker, not a bully, not greedy for money, but *hospitable,* loving what is good, sensible, righteous, holy, self-controlled" (emphasis added).

This book is for those church members who really want to see their churches make a difference.

A TALE OF TWO GUESTS

The stories are true. Only the names have been changed. Here are two doses of reality, and the first one is positive.

Jane is a stylist. She cuts hair. On this particular day, she cut my hair. I often say I get my hairs cut rather than getting a haircut. I don't know why people use the latter term. After all, who gets just one hair cut?

I am an introvert. If introversion were a spiritual gift, it would be my dominant spiritual gift. I would rather work in a room alone than work in a room with people I hardly know.

But I can't let my introversion be an excuse to be a silent witness. So I make myself come out of my shell. It's not just the right thing to do; it's Great Commission obedience.

As Jane was cutting my hairs, I began a conversation about her life and her world. Once I found out where she lived, I was able to shift the conversation to Jesus and church. Indeed, I found out she lived near my church where my son pastors.

So I talked to Jane about her life. I talked a bit about Jesus. And I invited her to church.

She was non-committal. Or so I thought.

Little did I know that the Holy Spirit had already been working in her life. I will spare you the details, but she soon found the website of our church and "bravely" (her word, not mine) decided to visit.

She "fell in love with the church" (her words again). The website gave her all the information she needed. She found the guest parking spot with ease. The people were genuinely friendly. The preacher preached the Bible with conviction and love.

I will cut to the chase: Jane decided to follow Christ. She was baptized.

And now she is smiling, enthused, and an active member of the welcome team ministry of our church.

Great story, huh? Well, let me share another story, one that is not so great.

His name is Ryan. I met Ryan in a consultation for a church where we focused on the guest experience. We had a one-hour in-person interview with him. And he let us have it!

Ryan had almost no church background. But I could tell he was really searching. So he did something bold, if not audacious, from his perspective. He asked his wife, Bethany, if she and their two young daughters would go to church with him.

Bethany had a nominal church background, but she was not really interested in going back to a church. She found the world outside the church more pleasant than church life. She nevertheless agreed to go with Ryan "just one time."

And there won't be a second time at the church they visited.

To begin, the church website was terrible. It had not been updated with the new time of the worship service. So the family of four was late, even though they thought they would arrive on time.

Because they arrived late, church members occupied all of the closer parking spots. Supposedly, there were guest parking spots, but Ryan could not find any directional signs to them.

When they arrived late, a couple of front door greeters spoke to them for at least two seconds. The two greeters then resumed their private conversation, oblivious to the world and people around them.

And when they went to the children's area to check in their two young daughters, disaster struck. The place was dirty. Security was weak. And the person that met them complained because they were late!

Bethany gave Ryan "the look." It was not a happy moment.

I'm surprised they even went into the worship service at this point. They both realized they made a bad decision.

I won't give you all the details of their experience. We will save these types of stories for later chapters. But, to state it plainly: it was not good.

By the way, when we interviewed members of this church, they consistently proclaimed a similar message: *Our church is very friendly!* And their church is friendly—as long as you know people. As long as you are on the inside. As long as you are not a guest.

By the way, Bethany and Ryan had a big fight on the way home from church. They were not happy campers. Ryan told us he would never return to that church. In fact, he told us he would never go to church again.

Sadly, I believe him.

THE MYTH OF THE WELCOMING CHURCH

Therein lies the problem with most churches. Churches perceive they are a friendly church because the members are friendly to one another. But they don't think about walking in the shoes of first-time guests. They don't look at their facilities, their parking, their website, or their friendliness from a guest perspective.

We learned not to ask church members if their church is friendly to find out if their church really is friendly.

Most church members have forgotten what it's like to be a first-time guest. They now have established relationships in the church. They love their church. Their biases tell them their church is great.

But many church members and leaders are wrong. When we asked hundreds of guests about their experiences visiting churches, it was not a pretty picture. We asked specifically why they did not return to a particular church. Here were their top ten responses:

1. *The stand-and-greet time in the worship service was unfriendly and awkward.* When I first saw this response coming in by the hundreds, I was surprised. And as I dug deeper, I discovered there were two issues

with the stand-and-greet time. First, some guests just felt awkward with the exercise. It seemed to be a ritual more for the members than the guests. Second, a number of guests did not mind the stand-and-greet time, but they felt left out during the welcome. Either they were totally ignored, or they were inundated with what they perceived were superficial greetings. I'll unpack this issue more in the next chapter.

2. *Unfriendly church members.* Most church members do not view themselves as unfriendly. But they do not see themselves from the perspective of church guests. They don't usually speak to guests because they don't know them. And the church members usually retreat to the comfort of the holy huddles of the people they do know.
3. *Unsafe and unclean children's areas.* This response generated the most emotional comments. If your church does not have clear safety and security procedures, and if the children's area does not appear clean and sanitary to the guests, do not expect young families to return to your church. Indeed, as word about your children's area grows, do not expect young families to visit the first time.

4. *No place to get information on the church.* Guests are trained by their experiences to look for a central welcome and information center. But here is the catch. Some churches did not have any such information center. Some churches did have them, but you couldn't find them. And some churches have them in good visible locations, but they had no one manning the welcome center. Guests told us they were hesitant to go to an unmanned welcome center. The church might as well not have an information and welcome center if no one will be there to help guests.
5. *Bad church website.* Nearly all the church guests checked the church website before they attended a worship service. Even if they decided to visit the church after looking at a bad website, they visited the church with a negative disposition. The two critical items guests want to see on a church website are the physical address of the church and times of the services. It's just that basic. Keep in mind this reality. The church website is now the front door of the church. Will guests feel welcome when they come to your front door? We will look at this issue in detail in chapter 3.

6. *Poor signage.* If you have been attending your church a few weeks, you don't need signage. But guests do. And they get frustrated when they don't have clear directional signage for parking, for the entrance to the worship center, for the children's area, and others. We will look at this issue more fully in chapter 3 as well.
7. *Insider church language.* Listen to the words in the worship service of your church. Listen to the announcements. Listen to the sermon. Listen to the casual conversations. Are members saying things that a first-time guest would not understand? Well, that's what church guests told us. They said they left some churches thinking that much of the language was foreign and filled with acronyms.
8. *Boring or bad church services.* My surprise was not that this factor made the top ten; it was that it was only listed as the eighth most frequent concern. In the past, church leaders of small churches would tell me they didn't have the resources for quality services. In the digital age, with so many affordable resources, no church is allowed that excuse.
9. *Members telling guests they were in the wrong pew or chair.* I thought this rude and insensitive behavior

disappeared years ago. The church guests told us otherwise. In fact the most common comment was, "You are sitting in *my* pew." Unbelievable. Totally unbelievable.

10. *Dirty facilities.* Some of the comments were brutal: "Didn't look like it had been cleaned in a week." "No trash cans anywhere." "Restrooms were worse than a bad truck stop." "Pews had more stains than a Tide commercial." You get the picture. A dirty church communicates to the guest, "We really don't care."

THE HAPPY GUESTS

To be fair, in our study of first-time church guests, we heard from a number of them who had really pleasant experiences, and decided to return. Let's look at the top ten responses from the perspective of the happy guest. Some of them are just the opposite of the ten items listed above. I have included in this list direct quotes from the happy guests.

1. *Someone asked the guest to sit with her.* "You know, as a single person, I can feel pretty lonely sitting by myself. I am so glad Joanie asked me to sit with her. We plan to get together for coffee."

2. *People introduced themselves to the guests.* "Several people introduced themselves to me. I did not get the impression it was either contrived or routine."
3. *There was clear signage.* "From the parking lot to the children's area to the worship center, everything was clearly marked. It was easy to navigate."
4. *There was a clearly marked welcome center.* "It made it really easy for me to ask questions and to get some information on the church."
5. *The kids loved the children's area.* "My kids were so happy with their experiences. We will be back for sure."
6. *The children's area was secure and sanitary.* "That is one of the first things I check when I go to a church. This church gets an A+!"
7. *Guest parking was clearly visible.* "From the moment we drove into the parking lot, I could find the guest parking. It was marked very well."
8. *The church did not have a stand-and-greet time.* "My wife and I just moved to the area and are visiting churches. If we visit one with that fake stand-and-greet time, we don't return."

9. *The members were not pushy.* "They seemed to really care about us rather than just making us another number on the membership roll."
10. *The guest card was simple to complete.* "*Some* of the cards in other churches ask for too much information. This one was perfect and simple."

Which list more accurately describes your church? Be careful and honest before you respond. About eight of ten guests had an experience that would better fit the unhappy guest category.

And sadly, few church members recognized it in their own churches.

So the first step in becoming a welcoming church may be the admission that your church may not really be a welcoming church.

Are you facing reality in your church?

··· POINTS TO PONDER ···

1. Why would guests and church members have such different views about the friendliness of a church?
2. When is the last time you spoke with a guest about his or her first-time visit to your church?

3. Look at your church website from a guest perspective. Be brutally honest with what you see. Is it guest friendly?
4. Do you think members in your church regularly invite guests? Why or why not?
5. How do you think a guest feels in your worship services? Explain with a bit of detail.

CHAPTER 2

I got in trouble not too long ago.

I wrote a blog post at ThomRainer.com on the well-worn "stand-and-greet" time in many churches across the globe. Some have other names, like "passing the peace." But the essence of the traditions is the same. It is a time when church members are supposed to greet guests and each other in the worship services.

Okay, I'm not a big fan of the stand-and-greet. My biases are evident when I write about it. It's probably a factor of my introversion. So, when I write about this practice, my biases are not well hidden.

But I made a lot of church members mad. I made some of them really mad. They love their stand-and-greet time. They did not like my opinion one bit, and they let me know it. So

I conducted a survey of both members and guests about this issue. I will let you know what I learned later in this chapter.

For now, I want you to join me as I share the results of our surveys to church guests on a wide variety of issues. For you statistical nerds, my surveys were done on social media, so the sampling was not precise. But, because of the huge numbers of responses I got, I am convinced the information was invaluable.

Here is the essence of what I found: we church members are often clueless about what our guests are thinking and experiencing. We think we know because we know how *we* feel and think. But the perspectives of church members and guests are often vastly different.

So let me share some of the surprises I learned from my foray into the world of church guests. Frankly, after I read their responses and rationale, I was surprised that I was even surprised.

THE WORST PART OF THE GUEST EXPERIENCE TAKES PLACE RIGHT BEFORE THE WORSHIP SERVICE BEGINS

Most of you have been a guest at a church. So let's replay the likely journey of visiting a church together. Keep in mind, this journey is especially important if you are looking at this church as a possible new church home.

Joining us on this journey are Kathy and Jim. They will be our guides because they are the ones who actually helped me visualize the issue not too long ago.

Kathy and Jim really needed a good guest experience. They had a lot of frustration getting their three kids, all under the age of eight, ready for church. To exacerbate the tension, neither Kathy nor Jim had been in a church for a decade.

They did not know what to expect.

Fortunately, the church they were visiting had its act together . . . mostly. You'll understand my caveat in just a few paragraphs.

"They had a great website," Kathy told me. "I was able to learn a lot about the church. I got the kids registered online so I didn't have to worry about the paperwork when I got to the church. Really, everything we needed to know was on their website."

Jim added, "Getting to the church from the street and in the parking lot was a breeze. The church had great signage everywhere. We were able to find the parking spots for guests in no time."

"I think the people were genuinely friendly," Kathy added. "They had real smiles on their faces. They greeted us warmly in the parking lot and when we entered the building. And folks were really helpful getting our kids to their areas."

Kathy paused then added, "We really had an overall good experience. But, there was one part that just was not that good. It was the nine to ten minutes after we sat down in the worship center and before the services started. No one spoke to us. No one sat by us. No one even acknowledged us. It was really uncomfortable until the service began."

That, in essence, is one of the surprises we heard from guests. Even in incredible churches, very few members make the effort to greet and speak to someone already seated before the service begins. And, frankly, most church members don't ever go sit with guests.

Guests are most often overlooked in the few minutes right before the worship services. No one speaks to them or sits with them.

VERY FEW CHURCHES CONSIDER GUESTS DURING THE STAND-AND-GREET

Let's return to the hot button issue. In my survey of church guests and church members on this topic, there were really divergent perspectives between the two groups.

Both a majority of the members and a majority of the guests would like to see the stand-and-greet time go away. For the members, about six out of ten really did not like it. But, to state it positively and fairly, four out of ten church members do like the stand-and-greet.

Here, however, is where the alarms began to sound. Nine out of ten guests do *not* like the stand-and-greet time in church services! What is that? Why are there such major differences between the preferences and opinions of the members and the preferences and opinions of the guests?

The guests addressed this issue in near unanimity. The stand-and-greet time is a tradition or ritual for the members, they told us. Members tend to greet other members they knew. Relationship patterns were obvious, and guests were on the outside looking in.

In some churches, however, the members did greet the guests. But, according to our survey, the greetings seemed artificial or contrived. "They greeted me because they were told to greet me," one respondent told me. "They never made an effort to say a word to me until their pastor commanded them to move."

Is it possible, then, to have a stand-and-greet time in the worship services that truly makes the guests feel welcome? My response is a tepid, "Maybe." It would mean that your members would need clear and firm guidance on specifically reaching out to guests. They would need to be friendly to them before and after the service. The members must be aware that friendliness only during the stand-and-greet time does more harm than good.

In all fairness, the motives behind the stand-and-greet time are probably good. But too many churches are not considering how guests feel during this time. Friendliness, for them, cannot be limited to two minutes of handshakes, smiles, and contrived exuberance.

For those of you reading who would say, "Well, we don't do the stand-and-greet time in our church, so we are off the hook," I would say, "Well, maybe." Perhaps you visit communion stations at your church during the service, and you float by guests like they are invisible. Or perhaps before and after the service, the culture of the church is to form discussion groups, boxing out folks who are new to your community. If that is the case, you share the same ailment.

MANY GUESTS SEE AN ABUNDANCE OF HOLY HUDDLES IN CHURCHES

The church I was consulting had an attendance of seven hundred. Part of my role was to get among the people as anonymously as possible before, during, and after the worship service. The experience was mostly good. The church had many positive and exciting things taking place.

But, like so many churches I have visited or consulted, they have a similar challenge, a challenge I call the "holy huddle." The holy huddle takes place when members talk to other members they know without acknowledging the people they don't know.

I get it. Members like to have fellowship and have conversations with friends they know. It's healthy to see these connections in a church.

But let me continue the story of my visit to the church. I gave you the attendance so you could get the context of my experience. When I was in the parking lot, I noticed two men with vests talking to each other. They were obviously part of the welcome team and greeter ministry. One of them did wave at me, but they then continued their conversation with each other.

I had never counted "holy huddles" before, but this time my curiosity got the best of me. By the time I walked from the church parking lot to several different places in the church building, I counted twenty-seven holy huddles! Of a total attendance of seven hundred, of which about five hundred were adults, people formed twenty-seven huddles.

Here is the challenge. These holy huddles are not intrinsically bad. To the contrary, they demonstrate life, fellowship, and healthy relationships. You certainly don't want a church where the members are not speaking to one another.

But, in twenty-six of the twenty-seven huddles, no one took time to acknowledge my presence. No one looked me in the eye. None of them stopped me to introduce themselves. The lone exception was the parking lot huddle, where one of the attendants waved to me. I think that was his job assignment.

The purpose of this book is not to break up fellowship groups; the purpose is to give church members awareness that the vast majority of guests feel like they are intruding on a party to which they were not invited.

I did see a healthy exception to this pattern in another church recently. I was the guest preacher, and a huddle had formed around me to welcome me and speak to me. But an elder broke out of my huddle with these words, "Excuse me, Thom, I don't recognize that couple over there. Let me go speak to them."

And that's the way it's done.

"WHERE'S THE BEEF?"

In 1984 the hamburger chain Wendy's introduced a commercial that became an instant classic. In the early releases, the commercial portrayed an elderly woman looking at a hamburger from a competitor of Wendy's. The meat in the burger was ridiculously small. So she yelled with frustration, "Where's the beef?"

Wendy's, of course, was making a point. The beef at their restaurants was bigger and fresher than the beef at other fast-food franchises. If you really wanted beef, you went to Wendy's.

This chapter is about surprises, things that church members may not consider about guests. One of those surprises was a figurative cry from church members: "Where's the information?"

Many guests want to get more information about the church they are visiting. While they may have gotten some information on the website, their visit indicates an even greater interest. They are looking for information. Can they find it at your church? Many of them told us they could not.

So here is a simple solution for churches of all sizes. Have a centrally located place where there is an abundance of information about the church. Call it a welcome center or guest center or information center—just have something.

Make it simple, but attractive. Have information available about the church. Have Bibles to give away. Have other gifts to give. Make certain you have a friendly and knowledgeable person manning the center any time there are guests in the church. Make certain that person does not get lost in a holy huddle.

It's very simple. Guests are internally exclaiming, "Where's the information?" Our churches must be able to respond with answers, resources, and clarity.

By the way, this guest center, or whatever you call it, is really important. In fact, it is so important that your signs should point to it.

THE SILENT KILLERS

Let me take you on one of my early church consultation experiences. Like many consults in my early years of working with churches, my learning curve for this consultation was steep.

The particular assignment for which I was retained was to help the church learn why many first-time guests were not returning. The church had many positive aspects to it. This lack of retention of guests confused the leadership of the church.

My process was simple. I personally interviewed twenty-four first-time guests who had not returned. Most of them were gracious to share their experiences at the church with me.

To be certain, as I went down my template checklist of questions, I received a lot of positive feedback. The people were very friendly. The lead pastor's sermons received rave reviews. The signage was clear and simple. And they were able to find the welcome center, the children's area, and the worship center with ease.

I remember vividly my internal reaction in the first interview. This lady, I thought, really liked the church. Her answers seem to contradict her actions. Why didn't she return after the first visit?

Well, my final question should get to the bottom of this enigma: What are the reasons you did not return?

Silence.

Hesitation.

So I asked the question again, in the unlikely event she had not heard me the first time.

She did answer this time. Both her response and hesitancy surprised me. She told me she did not return because the worship center was too dark. She could not read her Bible. She could not see other people well.

Indeed, as I interviewed all twenty-four of the guests, this issue and sound problems came up all but three times. Of this small sample, nearly nine out of ten of the first-time guests did not return because they struggled with either the sound or lighting in the worship service.

As I conducted hundreds of consultations over the next three decades, I heard many first-time guests mention the issues of light and sound. And while it's not a challenge in all churches, the issue was sufficiently pervasive to deem it important.

Sound and lighting.

Color me surprised.

In the event you are wondering why guests are hesitant to mention their problems with sound and lighting, I asked them. And they told me clearly. There were two common responses.

First, they felt petty by mentioning it. Here is my best recollection of the words from my first interview with Linda. "I hate even saying it," she began. "But I just have trouble worshipping when it's so dark I can't even see my Bible. I know I sound petty by saying it. I know there are a lot more important things than how bright the lights are. It's really not a gospel issue."

But she didn't return to the church. Nor did the others in my interviews.

The second issue was even a greater embarrassment to most of the guests. They felt like they were acting old or hyper-traditional by mentioning either sound or lighting. Note these words from Melvin, another first-time guest who did not return: "I just didn't want to come across as an old fuddy-duddy, but I guess I am."

I, indeed, was surprised. I was surprised that sound and lighting were so important that they hindered guests' return to the church. And I was surprised how difficult it was to get the guests to articulate their concerns.

It is the silent killer for getting guests to return.

You probably won't know about it unless you really ask a lot of questions. But the extra effort is well worth the time.

TOO FRIENDLY

About one out of seven guests told us, surprisingly, they did not return because the people were too friendly. Some noted that issue in the context of the stand-and-greet time, while others said it was an issue at all points in the church.

"I came away worn out from the visit to the church," Justin told us. "The people were all over us. My wife and I and our two kids were one of very few young families there, and they seemed desperate to get us. We left asking ourselves, 'Who are these people?' We had seen some of them in town, and they sure weren't friendly there. But they put on a good show when we visited."

Justin's comments about this church were common among those who shared this reason for not returning. The churches most often were older, established churches where the attendance has been declining and the median age has been increasing. For some of these churches, their friendliness comes across as either disingenuous or desperate or both.

WHAT'S NEXT?

Sometimes I am surprised how serious guests are about learning about the churches they are visiting. Many of them really desire to see if the church is a place for them and their families.

I shouldn't be surprised. Some of these guests are not Christians; they are really struggling with matters of the faith. Their visit is a clear indicator of the work of the Holy Spirit in their lives. They are seeking answers, and your church is a place they have come to get answers.

Other guests are believers, but they are making decisions about the church where they and their families will invest their lives. For committed believers, decisions about where they will go to church are not trivial issues.

So I should not be surprised that one of the challenges many guests expressed was the lack of clarity about next steps. Where can I get more information about the church? What are the next steps to becoming a part of the church? What are ministries that would impact my family and me?

In simple terms, what's next?

Every church should have clarity toward answering this question. Every guest should know what's next before he or she leaves the church grounds. And every guest should receive some type of follow-up within a short time, hopefully within twenty-four hours.

Many guests really want to know, "What's next?"

Is your church ready to answer them?

FROM LESSER KNOWNS TO MORE KNOWNS

The issues in this chapter were some of the surprises we found as we have surveyed and interviewed guests for the past three decades. Some of them have changed over the years. Most of them have not.

As we transition to some of the more commonly known guest issues in congregations, please read the information closely, carefully, and prayerfully. At the risk of overstatement, many of these issues have made life-changing, gospel-impacting differences in the lives of guests.

If you truly want to declare your church to be a welcoming church, you must put forth the prayerful effort to do these things we advocate. They are not merely methodological issues; they are gospel issues.

Read on.

It's really that important.

··· POINTS TO PONDER ···

1. Review each of the surprises in this chapter. Which of the surprises might apply to your church?
2. What are ways your church can help answer the question, "What's next?" to your guests?

3. Look at Hebrews 13:2: "Don't neglect to show hospitality, for by doing this some have welcomed angels as guests without knowing it." Relate this verse to some of the topics in this chapter.
4. Read 1 Peter 4:9: "Be hospitable to one another without complaining." What is the significance of the last two words: "without complaining"?
5. What can you do personally to make guests feel more welcomed just prior to the beginning of the worship services?

CHAPTER 3

I love GPS navigation.

Really. I wouldn't leave home without it.

You see, I traveled about two hundred days a year for a decade. It was a grueling schedule. Though I still travel a bit, it's nothing like those days where I was metaphorically walking barefoot in the snow.

My most painful memory was flying into Chicago where the arrival time was supposed to be 9:00 p.m. Because of bad weather, my flight was delayed, and I did not arrive until midnight. But that's just the beginning of the story.

My speaking engagement was in a town about two hours southeast of Chicago. So, after getting my rental car, I was hoping to arrive by 2:30 a.m.

Not.

My GPS system was typed directions and a paper map. I won't bore you with how many turns I missed in the darkness, but I arrived at the hotel at 4:00 a.m.

I didn't bother going to sleep since I had breakfast with my conference host at 6:30 a.m. I really was not my best that day.

We all need directions. Because navigation systems are so ubiquitous, we often take good directions for granted. But all of us have been frustrated when we did not know how to get somewhere.

Guests who visit your church need good directions. If they don't have clarity on how to get to your church buildings, and how to find areas once they arrive, they may not return. They may miss an opportunity to hear the gospel. You get the picture. It's just that important.

Before we look at this matter more deeply, let's deal with some common myths about good signage and websites. You may believe these myths yourself.

FIVE MYTHS ABOUT CHURCH SIGNAGE AND WEBSITES

I have consulted with hundreds of churches. One of the most common first steps I take is dealing with myths in churches. And myths about signage and websites are pervasive.

Here are five of them:

Myth #1: Everyone knows where our church is. No, they don't. I have been in retail establishments across the street from a church, and the clerk could not tell me where the church is located. In fact, most of the time, they've never heard of the church. I have been in churches in small communities where you assume everyone knows where everything is. They don't. It is an elitist attitude to assume everyone knows about your church.

Myth #2: Our church is small. We don't need signs for people to get around. Wrong again. Your guests don't know where to take their children. Your guests don't automatically know where guest parking spots are. And your guests really don't know where the restrooms are. Don't assume your small size lets you off the hook. It doesn't.

Myth #3: Church websites are really not that important. Whenever I hear that statement, I am tempted to scream. Of course, I don't, but the temptation is there. Please hear me clearly and carefully: most guests go to your church website before they ever set foot on your church property. What they find on the website could very well determine if they will be your guests or not. It's just that important. I'll address this issue in more detail later in this chapter.

Myth #4: It's easy to get around in our church. True story. I had a friend over to my home recently. Before he left, he asked to use my bathroom. Of course, I told him it was fine. For a few seconds, he just stood there. Of course, he did not know where the bathroom was located. My friend had never been to my home, and he did not know how to get around. Do you know why it's so easy to get around in your church? Because you go there. You worship there. You mingle there. You have years of familiarity with your church facilities. Your guests do not.

Myth #5: Signs and websites are human-centered methodologies. They are not central to the gospel. Sigh. I get it. A church sign is not a gospel essential. It is nothing compared to the centrality of Scripture. But why do we have to make such either/or choices? Look, heating and air conditioning are not central to the gospel. Why don't you just do away with them? These may not be issues of the first order, but that does not deem them unimportant. God has gifted us with these technological advances. We should steward them well.

A PRIMER ON CHURCH SIGNAGE

Good church signage is a statement of your church's hospitality. It means you are expecting guests; and it means you desire for guests to come to your church.

Bad or no church signage is a clear sign of a lack of hospitality. It means you are not expecting guests, or you don't care enough to get ready for guests. It means your congregation is focused on itself instead of others.

So let's take the signage issue seriously. Let's see what we can do to become a more welcoming church. Let's put ourselves in the shoes of others who have never visited our church. And let's go through a checklist to make sure our signs really communicate that we are ready to welcome guests.

What are some key signage issues a church needs to consider to be a hospitable church? Though this list is not exhaustive, it is a good checklist and beginning point.

✓ *Signage is not for members.* Remember, signage is not for church members on the inside; it is for those who are on the outside, many of whom have never visited your church. Strive to have "outsider eyes" when evaluating your signage. Think of that single mom with three small kids. Think of that couple coming to your church for the first time in their marriage. Think of that single man who is looking to your church for the first time as a church home. Look beyond yourselves. Serve beyond yourselves.

✓ *Quality signage is very important.* You don't have to spend a ton of money to get quality signage. There are many good and inexpensive sources to find high quality material. And, at the risk of being a grammar cop, please use good grammar on your signs. People do notice. And they think your church really does not care if your signs look cheap, or if someone did not take time to proofread the verbiage. I saw a sign recently with this message under the church's name: "Welcome Back from Spring Brake." Yes. Really.

✓ *The primary external church sign is also very important.* Many times zoning authorities will have specific restrictions on the size and type of signage. If there are no zoning restrictions, the main church sign should still complement other signage on the street. It certainly needs to be visible; but it should not look gaudy and out of place.

✓ *The parking lot should have clear signage.* Guests need to know exactly where to park. There should be clear traffic flow signage if needed. Even smaller churches need at least one sign to direct guests.

✓ *There should be clear signage pointing to the entry point or entry points of the church.* This issue is taken for granted in most churches, but guests tell us it is very important to their overall experience. Simply stated, guests want to know where to enter the church when they get out of their cars.

✓ *The two "must" signs are for handicap and guest parking.* The church may also, depending on its congregational makeup, have signs for senior adult parking, expectant mothers' parking, and parking for families with preschoolers, to name a few.

✓ *Internal signage must have three basic characteristics: good quality, readable font, and right height.* We see a number of churches that do not take into consideration the line of sight of guests. Often signs are either too high or too low to be seen easily.

✓ *All signage should be friendly and communicate an attitude of hospitality.* The following message we spotted on a sign posted outside a church's worship center did not communicate friendliness or joy: "Those bringing food or drink into the worship center will be asked to leave." Ouch.

✓ *Mobile signage can be very helpful for guests and for the church.* Many churches, for example, don't have the same parking requirements during the week as they do during weekend worship services. Mobile signage can be uniquely used for just the worship services.

✓ *Church leaders should conduct a signage audit at least once a year.* Some of the church leaders or members should inspect every external and internal sign for quality and relevance. Over half of the churches we have visited have internal signage to places that no longer exist or are in different locations now. Ouch again.

Before you dismiss this list as trivial or inconsequential, remember the biblical admonitions on hospitality. These signs are one key part of communicating true hospitality. And they could ultimately be a part of God's plan for gospel conversations to take place. It's just that important.

What if you volunteered, with the help of craftsmen in the church, to build, paint, or touch up signage at your church? What if, as a first step, you formed a group to brainstorm economically feasible ways to develop well-made signs for your church? Everyone can play a part; you don't have to be the executive pastor to be a welcoming church member.

THE FRONT DOOR WE OFTEN FORGET

What led you to visit our church?

The question began as an innocent conversation starter. I ask guests questions about themselves and their families. I do my best to get to know them, and to make the conversation about them. But, at some point, my curiosity gets the best of me. Out of the dozens of churches near them, what was the main factor that prompted them to try our church?

The answer still surprises me. "We visited the church's website."

We now hear that response from approximately seven out of ten first-time guests. Guests use Google to search for local churches, and they look at different church websites. They see the church sign driving by, and decided to look up the website. They hear a conversation about the church, and check it out by visiting the website. They are undecided about which church to visit, so they visit the website to check the service times and to see how long the drive would be.

Pause for a moment. Take in the reality of this objective and anecdotal research. Read these words again, this time very carefully: *Seven out of ten guests will go to a church website as a determinative factor in where they will choose to visit.*

While the website may not be the sole determinative factor, it's a determinative factor seven out of ten times.

In other words, if you aren't focusing resources and time on your church website, you are thumbing your nose at the Great Commission. And that's not an overstatement. A church with a lousy website is committing the sin of Great Commission negligence.

It's never been easier and more affordable to have a quality website as it is today. And your potential webmaster may be someone who is still a teenager!

Okay, if the church website is truly the front door of the church, how do we make the front door the most accessible? Over the past few years, my team and I have looked at hundreds of church websites. We found several recurring and common mistakes, particularly from a guest point of view. Jonathan Howe wrote about the following church website challenges at ThomRainer.com.

Address and worship times difficult to locate. This mistake is the most common reason a guest decides not to come to your church after he or she looks at your website. They won't come to your church services if they don't know the time of your services. And they won't come to your church services if they can't find a physical address to put in their GPS. We continue to be confounded by the number of church websites that do not give these items a clear and prominent place on the homepage of the site. And we are even more confounded when they aren't there at all.

Outdated information. True story: as I am writing this chapter, it is autumn. I went to a church website earlier this week only to discover the times of its special Easter service five months earlier! Seriously, I actually went to that church website because a friend texted me about it. His family had moved to a new city, and they were making decisions on where they would visit churches. This website was the third site they checked. It will not be one of the churches they will visit.

Lack of clarity about beliefs or doctrine. Not all guests will check this important item, but many will. Churches should not hesitate to share with clarity what they believe, particularly their core beliefs. Some of the most effective means to communicate doctrine begin with a simple link on the home page that says: "What We Believe." Those who choose to view the doctrinal statement can click to a full page of the church's basic beliefs. You may lose as many as half of your potential guests without this item.

Incomplete or total lack of information about children's ministry or student ministry. Parents want to know what the church has for their children. They not only want to know about ministries and activities, they want to know their children will be safe and happy when they come to your church. If you really want to win over these parents, tell them explicitly on your website how you will make certain their kids will be safe and secure when they attend your church. And, as an added measure, allow them to check in their kids online before they visit.

Poor graphics and copyrighted images. If you are using photos from a standard Google search for images, stop it. There are many good places where your church can get quality images for a small cost or even free. We live in a visual world. When a guest visits your church's website for the first time, those photos will shout a loud message about how much you care for those who are not yet there.

Hardly visible contact information. Have you ever been to a website where you have experienced difficulty finding out how to contact someone? Don't let it happen at your church's website. Guests may have questions before they visit. Why would you want to make your contact information so obscure that it's almost invisible? Let people know how to get in touch with the right person at your church. And, by the way, make certain you have someone who's responsible for responding to them promptly.

No photos of pastor, staff, and other leadership. Let your guests know that your leaders are real people. Show photos of the staff so guests can recognize the leaders when they visit your church (don't use your wedding photo, or outdated photos that you prefer because you think you look better). Let them begin to get comfortable with the leaders through their photos even before they arrive.

Obviously this list is not exhaustive. Some churches do a very good job of sharing the gospel through a written presentation. Often it begins on the home page with a link to: "How Can I Become a Christian?" Many churches provide the recorded messages of their pastor or other teaching pastors. Though the numbers are not large, there are some guests who like to hear a sermon before they visit.

Simply stated, whether the matter at hand is the seemingly mundane issue of church signage or a good church website, we who serve in local churches should not take these matters lightly. They are clear messages about how much we really want guests to visit our church. They are messages of hospitality or the lack of hospitality. They demonstrate, at least from the guests' perspectives, whether you care about them or not.

A SAD BUT TRUE STORY

I met Ella during a series of interviews I was conducting for a church consultation. One of our assignments was to contact guests who came to the church but never returned. After I heard her story, I was amazed she even stayed for the service at her first visit.

Ella is married, but her husband does not attend church. The family was new in town, but Ella was determined to get her three children, all under the age of seven, back in church after two years of not attending.

She passed a church sign and noted it in her mind as a place to visit the next Sunday. She looked up the church on the website, found the time for the worship service, and planned to visit.

The website indicated the service started at 10:15. It actually started at 10:00. The time of the service was changed seven months earlier, but no one thought to change it on the website. So when Ella arrived at 10:05, she was five minutes late, not ten minutes early.

By the way, it started raining as she drove to church. She could not find any signs for guest parking, so she parked some distance from the church entrance. And she still moved forward in the rain with three young kids in tow.

Since she was late, she really didn't have anyone to follow into the church facility. So she went to the obvious front entrance . . . only to find the door was locked. Two of the children were crying and all of them were soaking wet, but Ella was determined. She finally found the right door.

By this time there were no greeters. There was also no signage to tell Ella where to take her children. Exasperated, but determined, she made three wrong turns in hallways but finally found the children's area.

She missed the first twenty minutes of the service, and she had trouble focusing for obvious reasons. Ella still completed a guest card and turned it in when the offering plate came by. She was curious if anyone would really contact her.

No one did. She was not surprised.

Ella was gracious but factual in her interview. She said unequivocally she had no plans to return to the church. Without my prompting, she offered some further counsel. She let me know she was a Christian, and that she and her children ultimately found a good church home.

But, she told me, if she were not a Christian, and if she had summoned the courage for only one church visit, she would have never returned to any church after her bad experience. Her final words are worthy of a direct quote.

"That church in everything it did—bad website, no signs inside or out, and no greeters around—sent me a clear message: 'Guests are not welcome here.' And if I had not been a Christian before I came to the church, I probably still would not be a Christian today."

It's not just about signs and sites, it's about the message of hospitality. And that message of hospitality becomes the pathway where we can share the message of the gospel with people.

That's why we must become welcoming churches.

··· POINTS TO PONDER ···

1. Look at the five myths about church signs and websites. Do you think any of those myths are in your church?
2. Review Romans 12:13, 1 Timothy 2:2–3, and Titus 3:7–8. As you see the repetition of the word *hospitable*, do you see your church's signage and website as truly hospitable?
3. Review your church's website again. Does it show clearly the most important information for guests?
4. Why does it matter if your church has its beliefs on the website?
5. Does the information in this chapter make you view your church differently? How?

CHAPTER 4

SAFE CHURCH / CLEAN CHURCH

It was my first church where I was the pastor.

I was excited beyond description. Not only was it my first church, it was the *only* church that did not reject me. Frankly, I don't remember how many churches rejected me during my seminary days. It was obviously more than I care to remember.

As just one painful example, I preached in a church that was interested in me. After I preached, the chairwoman of the search committee said to me, "I've heard a lot of bad sermons, but that was one of the worst. You need a lot of work before you pastor a church."

Ouch.

But before I go down an irrelevant path, let me get back to the story of my first church. The congregation had to vote on my call. The vote was an affirmation of 6 to 1.

Yes. That's right, there were only seven people in the church.

The negative voter hated my preaching (her words). The other six said they had no other candidates, so I was their only choice.

So much for an affirmation.

The first Sunday I was serving as pastor, I asked one of the members a pretty basic question: "Where is the restroom?" He did not answer. So I asked again. He looked down at the floor and, this time, responded meekly, "We don't have one."

First, how did I accept a call to a church without knowing there was no restroom? Obviously, I'm not the brightest bulb in the chandelier. Second, how does a church function without a restroom? I decided to ask the same member another question: "What do you tell guests who ask where the restroom is?" I asked.

He responded, "We don't have any of those."

I understood who "those" were. The church had no guests. They obviously expected no guests, and they were obviously not prepared for guests if they did come.

By the way, before I left that church, we had a "building program." That's right. We added a single restroom to the church. I remember the irony as we sang the dedication hymn for the new facility: "There Shall Be Showers of Blessing."

ARE YOU PREPARED?

Let me go back to two earlier sentences about my first church: *They obviously expected no guests. They were obviously not prepared for guests if they did come.*

Many of our churches look like they don't expect company. They may have seven hundred guests instead of seven, but they are sloppy. They are cluttered. They are not clean. And, many times, they are not safe.

When my mom was living, I visited her as often as I could, but sometimes the trips were infrequent. My wife and I had three young sons, and Mom lived ten hours away. So when I did get to her home, several weeks typically had passed.

Among the things I wanted to do for her while I was there were simple household chores like replacing light bulbs. And I would look for wear and tear and safety concerns she could have someone in the community handle.

But I noticed a pattern with each subsequent trip. I would ask Mom, for example, if she had noticed the step on the back porch that was cracked. She had not. I would point out some peeling paint she had not seen. The pattern continued.

You see, my mom saw the place every day, so she was unable to see it from an outsider's eyes. I was like the guest showing up for the first time. I noticed things those familiar with the place did not see. And what I saw made me cringe.

You may be too familiar with your church. You may have lost the ability to see things from an outsider's perspective. Or you may love your church so deeply that you are willing to overlook issues such as clutter or dirt or unsafe areas.

But your guests have a different vantage point. They know little or nothing about your church. They are receiving first impressions for those areas you no longer see. They are making decisions on whether they will return or not. Some of them may be making decisions that have an eternal impact.

Will your facilities say, "welcome" or "we don't care"?

There are two primary considerations for most guests: safety and cleanliness. Let's look at each of these.

THE SAFE CHURCH

My church's insurance company gave us a checklist of about 150 items to make certain that the church was a safe place for members and guests. I glanced at the list and saw things I would have never considered. For example:

- Are batteries for exit signs checked regularly?
- Is there proper illumination on stairways?
- Are rugs and mats in good condition or properly repaired?
- Is the right type of fire extinguisher visible and available?
- Are any electrical cords frayed, broken, or in some type of disrepair?
- Are there tripping hazards such as stumps or rocks?

You get the point. I am grateful for insurance companies that provide such exhaustive lists for churches. And I would encourage you to ask your church's insurance company for a safety checklist. And if they don't have one, you might not have the right insurance company.

But, for the purposes of guests, there are two primary and high-level issues to consider: safety and cleanliness. While these issues are important to all guests, they take on heightened importance if the guests include children.

THE SAFE CHURCH AND CHILDREN

"It will never happen in my church."

Those are the words a pastor shared with me. He told me he really believed those words. He thought such a tragedy would never happen at his church.

But it did.

The church is now involved in an awful and highly visible lawsuit. The allegations include negligence and sexual abuse of a child. It can happen.

Hear me clearly. The protection of our children is more than an issue of guest friendliness; it is absolutely necessary. But it does have significant application to guests for at least two major reasons.

First, there are a lot of those children. The Millennial generation, those Americans born between 1980 and 2000, is the largest generation in America's history. They are seventy-eight million strong. And though only about one out of four attend church with any degree of consistency, there are still almost twenty million or more who will show up at a church.

And guess who is coming to church with the Millennials? Their kids. Some call them Gen Z, and others call them iGen. In Jean Twenge's book, *iGen,* she describes this generation in this subtitle: "Why Today's Super-Connected Kids Are

Growing Up Less Rebellious, More Tolerant, Less Happy—and Completely Unprepared for Adulthood."

Whew. While the author offers some fascinating insights to the kids of this generation, one thing about them is totally clear: Their parents want them safe and protected wherever they are, including church.

While many Boomer kids were free to roam the neighborhoods and ride their bikes to school and the movies, the iGen kids are supervised at almost every moment. They are accustomed to car seats, ubiquitous seat belts, and sanitized plastic playgrounds. Their Millennial parents, for the most part, do not want them out of sight.

So if you really expect to see younger families visit your church, you absolutely must demonstrate that your church is safe, secure, and sanitary. In fact, I just spoke with a Millennial who told me she was not taking her kids back to a particular church because the toys were so unsanitary. "It was a literal breeding ground for germs and diseases," she told me. "I will never return there."

The second issue is safety, particularly safety from sexual predators. I get it. This issue is one churches must take with utmost care and seriousness. If your church brushes this issue aside, it does not deserve to have guests, or any children for that matter, attending. This issue is more than a guest issue, but it is also a guest issue.

Regardless of the size of your church, there should be certain rules that all churches follow regarding those who work with children. While we won't offer a comprehensive overview here, let's look at just some basic issues.

- Anyone who works with children should be required to be a member of the church for an established length of time.
- All children's workers should complete a written application.
- Regardless of how well you know the worker, everyone should be interviewed before working with children.
- Before someone works with children, they should be subject to reference checks, criminal background checks, and checked with the national sex offender registry.
- The church should maintain records for all children's workers.
- The church should have some type of ongoing training for volunteers and staff.

- The church should have a clear response plan to protect victims according to all applicable laws, in the event of an incident.
- The church should be certain that any off-campus small groups, regardless of where they meet, fall under these same guidelines.

Regarding the latter issue, I am familiar with more than one church that is now involved in a lawsuit because they did not require those who watched the children during an off-campus adult small group to follow the same guidelines for children's workers at the church facility.

Child sex abuse in churches has been the number one issue of litigation for churches for over two decades. More than ever before, parents are highly sensitive to this issue for their own children. And they should be.

In the previous chapter, we looked at the importance of websites for churches. But I rarely see a church that explains powerfully and clearly on their website how they protect children who come to the church. There are likely Millennial parents going to your church website every week to discern if their children would be safe and secure at your church. More churches should have a clear message of "How We Protect Your Children at Our Church" for parents to read on their website.

It is just as important, if not more so, than showing the times of worship services and the physical address of the church.

THE SLOPPY CHURCH

In a church consultation, I interviewed a man who was a first-time guest at the church just two days earlier. I asked him to share with me his first impression.

"Sloppy," he said.

I asked him for more details.

"The church looked like a disorganized yard sale," he continued. "There were old Bibles everywhere, including the restroom. And I guess a few dozen people forgot their umbrellas and coats, because they were strewn everywhere. And then there were the upright pianos."

"Upright pianos?" I asked.

"Yeah," he responded. "What is it with churches and upright pianos? I have visited several churches over the years, and I have seen several with old, ugly, unused upright pianos."

He's right. In our conversations with churches, that is something we see with frequency. In fact, when I mentioned it at a conference, an attendee sent me a photo of an upright piano in his church. It was in the men's restroom.

I had no words.

Keep in mind, the story I told you above was about a first-time guest. It was his impression of a church within two days after his visit. His one word first impression was telling: sloppy.

I asked him if he planned to return to the church. His response was kind but succinct: "I don't think so."

We have conducted hundreds of interviews with first-time guests like this man. And we hear similar themes. In one way or another, they articulate to us that churches look like they aren't expecting guests or they don't like guests. Here are some of the most common observations from these guests with a representative quote.

Clutter. "I felt like the place had become a storage house for everything members didn't want or forgot."

Scarcity of garbage cans. "I had an empty coffee cup in my hand when I entered the church. I took it home with me. I only found one trash can and it was overflowing."

Odors. "It was a weird musty smell. It reminded me of when my parents used to take me to visit my great-aunt. Her house was really dirty and always had a stale odor to it."

Unstocked restrooms. "I'm glad I checked all the stalls. There was no toilet tissue in any of them. I asked my husband to take me to McDonald's so I could find a clean and stocked restroom. We never made it back to the church."

Paper signage. "If we put such tacky signs up at my office, we would hear from someone right away. It just looked bad."

Out-of-date information. "I read about an upcoming mission trip. But the date on the trip was two months old. Then I read about the big Easter celebration that was to take place three months ago."

Dirty carpet. "I hope the church is giving a lot of money to missions, because they sure aren't spending it on carpet cleaning. It's gross."

Faded paint. "You know, almost any church can give the place a facelift with fresh paint. I just don't think this church gave a rip about the faded and peeling paint."

Torn and dirty pew cushions. "We found another row of pews. The first place we sat had torn and filthy pew cushions."

Poor lighting. "The place is dark and depressing, even in the main foyer where they are greeting people."

I could continue, but you get the picture. The sloppy church sends a message to the guests. It says we really don't care how this place looks, and we really don't care how it affects our guests. In reality these churches don't expect guests at all.

WHAT SAFE AND CLEAN CHURCHES DO

After several hundred consultations, I have seen a clear pattern with churches that are truly safe and clean. These are the congregations noticed by guests. These are the churches where guests desire to return.

As a prefatory note, I see no relationship in size of church and the safety and cleanliness of church facilities. There are good and bad examples among all sizes of churches. Similarly, no pattern exists related to the income level of churches.

It all comes down to having the right perspective, the right attitude, and the right effort.

They see the issue from a gospel perspective. Certainly the leaders of these churches desire clean and safe churches for the obvious reasons: they want a facility that is safe and clean. But they have a bigger vision than that. They realize many of the guests will not be followers of Christ. And if the leaders of the church can demonstrate they care about the safety of those who visit, those guests may very well return. And they could very well hear and respond to the gospel.

They find champions. A champion is a person who is both passionate and accountable about a ministry. I recently was in a small church that gave a great first impression. I learned later that a woman saw her ministry as one to keep the church as clean as possible. She found a team to help her with the tasks. As far as I could tell, everyone followed her lead, and saw their work as gospel ministry.

They focus on three distinct areas: cleanliness, safety, and security. And the best-in-class churches have champions for each of the areas.

They have regularly scheduled check-ups in all three areas. Many of these churches had checklists they used with a frequency of once a quarter to once a year.

They listen to a secret guest. I have come to expect guest-friendly churches to schedule a secret guest at least once a year. I have also been encouraged to see many of the leaders listen carefully to these guests to make improvements in the areas of cleanliness, safety, and security. And when they hear of an area in need of improvement, they act immediately.

They check out other churches. A church in the Southwest with an average worship attendance of 240 sends three or four "ambassadors" to other churches every quarter. They then report back their discoveries, and how they could use those discoveries to improve their own facilities, particularly in the areas of cleanliness, safety, and security.

We cannot discuss the issue of safety without mentioning the fear of church shootings in our culture. What does your church do to communicate clearly to guests that your church addresses this matter seriously? At my church we have a highly visible police car in the parking lot. And a plain clothes policemen with a visible gun and badge stands at the front entrance greeting people. We have heard from countless guests the security they feel when they see the police car and the policeman.

Frankly, the issue is simple. If churches really care, they will always strive to be clean and safe. It's not a matter of money; it's a matter of commitment and execution. And if your church is not clean and safe, it is a reflection of lack of attention at best, and a lazy and uncaring attitude at worst.

And from the guests' perspective, it's usually a deal breaker. I am amazed at how few church leaders and church members don't confront this reality. If you have guests who don't return, there is a reason. And that reason may be a church that seems to them to be sloppy, dirty, and unsafe.

The guests may think the church does not really care.

It really is a gospel issue.

It really is that important.

··· POINTS TO PONDER ···

1. If you were to rate the cleanliness of your church on a scale of 1 to 10, with 10 being highest, how would you rate it? If you did not rate it a 10, what improvements could be made?
2. How can cleanliness and safety be a gospel issue?
3. What do you think Millennial parents expect of a church facility when they bring their children to church? Does your church meet those expectations?
4. Has your church ever had a thorough safety inspection? What do you think the results are or would be?
5. Look at this verse in Colossians 3:23: "Whatever you do, do it from the heart, as something done for the

Lord and not for people." How would you relate this verse to the topics of this chapter? How should it affect your attitude as you seek to help make your church cleaner and safer?

CHAPTER 5

Steve had such a severe case of introversion that he made me look like an extrovert.

In case you have not heard, I am a pretty extreme introvert. I could be happy all day in a closed office. Yeah, I know. It's sad.

But Steve really had it worse than I do. He struggled to look people in the eye. He could not carry on a conversation with a stranger. He knew he was an introvert.

By the way, Steve was the first person I ever asked to be a greeter in the church.

It doesn't make sense, does it? Why would I ask one of the most extreme introverts I've ever known to be in a ministry requiring an outgoing personality?

The answer is simple. I was desperate.

My little church had grown to about twenty-five people, but everyone was really busy doing something at the church. Well, everyone was busy but Steve.

Steve was a new Christian. I was mentoring and discipling him. During one of those times of mentoring, I decided to go for broke. "Steve," I said, "you would do a great job becoming a greeter at our church."

I cannot communicate adequately the look on his face. It was something like, "You are crazy" and "You must be an alien from outer space." His response was swift: "No!" Actually he added a profane word to his rejection. God was still working on his sanctification.

I was not surprised. Indeed I would have been surprised otherwise. But I still needed a greeter at the church. I was still desperate.

One day I went to get Steve at the body shop where he worked on cars. We had gotten into a routine of my picking him up before we went to McDonald's for coffee and Bible study.

But this time I noticed something about Steve. He was engaged in a conversation with a lady about the repairs she needed on her car. I could tell she was really concerned about the cost of repairs. I watched in amazement as Steve calmed her nerves and told her how she could get by with a few affordable repairs.

When he got in the car, I stared at him and smiled. "What?" he asked in exclamation. "You dog," I said with affirmation. "You do just fine interacting with people. I saw how you handled that lady. She went from upset to calm in just a few minutes." Then I brought down the hammer: "You are now officially our greeter at the church."

While he offered me a few more unprintable words, I could see he was curious. "Look, man," I began. "Being a greeter just means being your friendly self, just like you were with that lady. You don't have to be someone you're not. Just pretend like you are at the body shop about to have a conversation with a customer."

No, Steve did not acquiesce immediately. But he did make the move eventually, "on a very trial basis," according to his stipulations. But he never left that ministry while I was at the church. And he became an incredible greeter, an incredible representative for Christ at our church.

And he even stopped cussing while he was greeting people.

WHY DO WE EVEN NEED GREETERS?

It's a fair question. Shouldn't we expect everyone in the church to be friendly to guests? Why do we have to ask people to do what they should be doing anyway? Perhaps in an ideal world with an ideal organization with ideal people such an approach would work. But that's not our world, and that's not our church. We, therefore, greatly need greeter ministries for three reasons.

It's a focused ministry. Many of our members are already involved in other ministries. The leaders who are checking in and caring for children can't go to the parking lot to greet people. The worship team that is making quick adjustments before the service begins can't drop what they are doing and become greeters at the doors. The Sunday school or small groups teacher is waiting on other group members to arrive. He can't leave the room and man the welcome center.

We need people in ministry whose sole focus at the moment is greeting people. We need church members who understand greeters do more than merely saluting people upon arrival; we need them to be praying about the encounters they will have each week. For some, they will have a divine encounter with a guest. That man or woman or child who is visiting your church comes with expectations and needs. The first line of ministry takes place with greeters.

Simply stated, the greeter ministry is too important to be a casual thought in church life. As I noted, I have been consulting with churches for over three decades. I see what an incredible difference a good greeter ministry makes. I know churches where the greeter ministry was used of God in part to bring a true transformation and revitalization to the congregation. And I know people who were not followers of Christ who were greatly influenced toward the gospel by greeters.

Our churches need greeters. Our congregations need to take seriously this ministry and make it a key part of the life of the church.

It moves people to strategic locations. Can you imagine walking into a restaurant to learn that the host or hostess is somewhere in the kitchen? Would you go looking for him or her if they weren't there to greet you?

A greeter is a leader in ministry. It is critical that these leaders are strategically located where they will make first and powerful connections with guests. When we have a good greeter ministry in our church, we know where every greeter will be. We know the specifics of every assignment.

You see, without an organized greeter ministry, we are not likely to be where the guests are. We are not likely to see them when they arrive.

It is not an overstatement to say the presence of greeters in strategic locations could very well have an eternal gospel impact on someone.

It's just that important.

It commits volunteers to specific times. The pastor contacted me with a sense of desperation. He asked me to conduct a consultation for the specific purpose of determining why guests showed up late for the worship services. It was a consistent and troubling pattern.

Children's workers were frustrated because they were signing in children of guests late. The workers were not able to begin the lessons on time for the other children. Greeters also had their challenges. They wanted to be on duty when guests arrived, but many of the guests were late. They too had to wait before they were able to go to the worship services.

The murmuring grew among the members as the pattern continued. So the pastor retained me for one of the most focused consultations I had experienced. "Please tell us," he said, "what options we have about guests who arrive late."

My process was simple. I would be among the greeters. When a guest arrived late, I would ask three or four brief questions, including a non-threatening question about their late arrival.

By Sunday afternoon, I had solved the mystery. The pastor thought I was a genius. His evaluation of me was overrated.

In fact, I knew the answer as soon as I spoke with the first late arriving guest. She told me she was not late. Confused, I looked at the church's website. The time of the service was incorrect! The church had its website re-done a few weeks earlier. In the process of revamping the site, the worship time was listed incorrectly by fifteen minutes. In fact, as I noted in an earlier chapter, I have seen this mistake more than once.

The pastor was embarrassed. I was thrilled. The problem was solved.

There are many lessons to this story, but let's focus on one of them. All the workers in the church were waiting on the guests, even to their own inconvenience. They wanted to be in the right place at the right time when guests arrived. Such is the encouragement I offered the pastor.

Among the many reasons we have a greeter ministry is to welcome the guests at the specific time they arrive. We want our churches to be welcoming churches, but we can't welcome people we miss. Greeters not only have specific places to be, they have specific times to be there.

Speaking of specific places, where are greeters stationed in the most effective welcoming churches? In the most effective churches, they are in at least six locations.

STRATEGIC LOCATIONS FOR GREETERS

Every church is different, so we should not presume a template approach to this issue is best for every congregation. But, in the most effective greeter ministries, we see a consistent pattern of where greeters are located.

The parking lot. For some reason, I have trouble convincing church leaders the importance of parking lot greeters. The excuses are common: "We are just a small church, we don't need greeters there." "The greeters wouldn't have anything to do."

"Our signs do the job; we don't need those greeters."

Parking lot greeters are essential. They form the first impression for guests. Their role may simply be to wave and smile. If necessary, they can provide directions to guest parking. They can offer assistance in inclement weather. They can hold car doors open for young parents unloading their kids. They can simply answer questions.

You see, your church is missing a prime opportunity to make a great first impression without parking lot greeters. But fewer than ten percent of the churches I consulted had them or even considered them.

The entrances. This one is obvious but often neglected. Churches need at least one greeter at every entrance where a guest might enter. But let me share where many churches miss the mark here.

First, they don't consider *all* of the entrances a guest might enter. Most churches have a primary entrance for worship services. Hopefully, there is clear signage to point guests in that direction. But I have been in many churches where some of the guests choose another entrance.

For example, I was at a church where the foyer to the worship center was the main entrance. Most of the guests came through the side door of the foyer facing the guest parking lot. But some of the guests came through the front door facing the street. Those guests who came through the side door were greeted warmly. But those guests who came through the street-facing doors were totally ignored.

For certain, this church was a friendly church. And this church would never intentionally ignore a guest. But they did. And I bet if you surveyed the ignored guests, you would see a return rate much lower than the other guests.

A second factor is not so obvious. We have found that if greeters at the entrances are on the outside of the entrance rather than the inside, guests respond more favorably. Guests have a particular trepidation as they enter a church facility. If they see outside greeters waiting for them, they become relaxed and encouraged.

Greeter location is indeed important.

The roaming greeter. Even though I am an introvert, I am on the welcome team at my church. So is Paul. I am a people-watcher, and I love to watch Paul in action as a greeter. His official role is "runner," which is another way of describing a roaming greeter. It is Paul's role to make certain no guests get overlooked.

For example, in the short walk from the front door to child registration at our church, guests often stand alone. They have been greeted in the parking lot. They have been greeted at the front door. But now they are inside the building waiting to register their children. Paul watches out for these guests. If they are alone, he engages them in conversation.

He simply makes certain all guests are welcomed at our church. And he does a very good job.

The worship center greeter. We've heard it repeated times. Guests feel most uncomfortable after they enter the worship center or sanctuary and sit down. No one speaks to them any longer. Typically no one sits with them. And because many of the members arrive late or right at the beginning of the service, the guests feel alone.

Such is the reason worship center greeters are important.

Think of them as roaming greeters in the worship services. They observe guests entering. They speak to them at the point of entry. But then they observe after the guests are seated. And if they see guests are ignored or uncomfortable, they engage them again while the guests are seated. In some churches, there are sufficient numbers of greeters to sit with the guests.

Remember, you are more likely to lose the favor of a guest once he or she enters the worship center. Don't let it happen in your church. Worship greeters will make a huge difference.

COMMON MISTAKES OF GREETERS

You have a big advantage.

You can learn from this book the mistakes other churches have made in their greeter ministries. And, in so doing, you can avoid some of the blunders and make your church's ministry one of the best. Here, then, are some of the most common mistakes of greeter ministries.

Holy huddles. I know. I am being redundant on this point. But it's just that important. If your church has two or more greeters conversing with each other as guests arrive, you are already excluding the guests. They are not a part of the conversation. They are not a part of the group. They feel left out.

Here is the reality: it is better to have no greeters at all than to have greeters in holy huddles. They are in their roles of ministry to serve the guests. So the guests deserve all of their focused attention. Break the holy huddles.

Arriving too late; leaving too early. Mike became the second greeter at my rural church in southern Indiana. He was blown away I asked him to serve. Our service started at 11:00 a.m. (surprise!), but Mike was always outside ready to greet by 10:30 a.m., even if no one had yet arrived.

I told Mike he did not have to be in his greeter role that early. He disagreed. In fact, he kind of chastised me. "Pastor," he said sternly, "I was serving in this spot when Hank arrived a few months ago. We started a great conversation. He began to feel okay about coming into the church. And you know the rest of the story. Hank got saved a few weeks later."

Mike paused for a moment. The intensity in his expression was strong. "So," he continued. "If getting here a few minutes early makes a difference in someone's eternity, I think it's a small price to pay."

I had no retort. He was right.

Greeters should be in their positions before the first guests arrive. And they should stay late, because as many as half of the guests will arrive late.

Be on time. Stay late. Heed Mike's words. Eternity could hang in the balance.

Calling the bulletin person a greeter. I'm still not sure what to call that person. You know, the person in many churches who hands you a bulletin or a worship folder or whatever you call it. Some call them ushers, but most of them don't really show people to their seats. I tried calling the role the bulletin-hander-outer-person, but it didn't catch.

Regardless of the name, please don't call them greeters. Yes, their role is important. And, yes, it likely includes some type of greeting. But the bulletin people don't have the capacity to engage people in conversation while fulfilling their other duties. Again, greeters need to be freed and focused to greet.

If these people are considered full-fledged greeters, someone will be missed. A guest will be neglected. The ministry is indeed important, but it's really not a greeter ministry.

Failing to introduce yourself. Greeters are real people. Guests are real people. When greeters introduce themselves to guests, they need to speak as if it is a normal encounter. When we meet someone for the first time, or greet them for a second time, we don't just shake their hands and walk away. We say something like, "Welcome! I'm Thom." It's pretty basic, but it makes a huge difference.

And if you are good at remembering names, use their names to speak to them and their children again later. It is a powerful act. Just make sure you get their names right. It can be powerful in the opposite direction as well.

THE WELCOME CENTER

Every church should have a welcome center. No exceptions. None.

The welcome center serves several purposes, but it should always be viewed from the perspective of the guest. With that in mind, here are some tips for an effective welcome center.

It can be simple. While some churches have fully built out welcome centers with counters, fixed signage, and lighting, it does not have to be elaborate. It can be a table with a tablecloth, some neat mobile signage, and adequate lighting.

It should be manned when guests are present. A welcome center is only an information center if no one is present. The person who mans the welcome center is typically a critical part of the greeter ministry. And he or she is typically a person with an outgoing and engaging personality. I have never been asked to man the welcome center at my church.

It should have information on the church. That information on the church may be redundant with the information on the church's website, but that's okay. We still have people who like to feel, touch, and keep information they can hold. A note of caution is in order here. The information grows stale and outdated soon. Check it every month to assure its timeliness and relevancy.

It should have gifts. Some churches offer Bibles. Some churches give away church mugs. Some churches provide a gift card to guests. I wrote the little book *We Want You Here* as an affordable giveaway for every guest. When a guest takes a gift home, he or she is more likely to return to the church. Gifts are really important.

It should have pens. The person manning the welcome center often needs to write information for the guests. And it is not unusual for the guests to write down information to leave with the church. Have pens they can take home and remember the church.

It may have treats. Different churches have different views on providing treats like candies. I get that. But if I get chocolate from the church, I'm not forgetting the church. In fact, I may return the next week just to get some more chocolate.

And then there's coffee. No welcome is complete without a lot of coffee for guests. In fact, I was at a church that did not have a coffee station. A first-time guest commented somewhat gruffly to a church greeter, "You don't have coffee? I thought all churches had coffee. What's wrong with you folks?"

Please don't forget the coffee.

THE FIRST IMPRESSION FACTOR

Greeters and welcome centers send a clear message to guests. They say with clarity "we are expecting you." They are critical to a guest's first impressions. In fact, what takes place in the few minutes from the time a guest drives on the campus until he or she sits down in the worship center shapes the first impression significantly.

Greeters and welcome centers, however, say even more. They don't just say, "We are expecting you," they say, "We want you here." And a guest who feels wanted and welcomed is a guest who will likely return. It is really that important.

··· POINTS TO PONDER ···

1. On a scale of 1 to 10, with 10 being the highest and perfect, how would you rate your church's greeter ministry according to the information in this chapter?
2. What changes could your church make to be closer to a perfect score?
3. In the early church culture, it was common to greet one another with a holy kiss, such as portrayed in 1 Thessalonians 5:26: "Greet all the brothers and sisters with a holy kiss." While not all cultures include the physical kiss in greeting, why do you think the Bible exhorts us to greet people at church?
4. Pretend you are a guest at your church for the first time. Does the signage clearly point you to where the entrances and greeters are?
5. Review and discuss the importance of the worship center greeter.

CHAPTER 6

Allow me to ask you a rhetorical question. Would you return to a place where you did not feel welcome?

I am not certain why some church leaders and members take it for granted that guests will come and stay with little or no effort on their part. Here is the reality: what takes place in the first ten minutes when a first-time guest arrives at your church will largely determine whether he or she returns.

Is it really that important? You bet it is! Let's see why.

GRASPING THE IMPORTANCE OF BECOMING A WELCOMING CHURCH

Here is the first step. You must understand and believe in the importance of becoming a welcoming church. If you don't buy in, you won't emphasize it. You won't lead it. You won't work it.

There are gospel realities to the welcoming church. You have read some of the stories in this book already. So please don't look at this issue as some mere methodological fix in your church.

Think about, for example, an unbeliever visiting your church. When non-Christians feel welcomed, they return. When they return, they have more opportunities to hear the gospel preached and to develop relationships with believers in the church. And those relationships are often used of God to bring people to His Son.

How many first-time guests do you estimate visit your church on the average every week? Let's assume the number is four, inclusive of all adults and children. That's the equivalent of just one family. Now do the math. Four first-time guests a week equal more than two hundred a year!

I visited a church with an average attendance of 280. They monitored their numbers and found that they averaged six first-time guests. Typically it was one or two families each week. They were blown away when they realized they had over 300 guests a year!

But it's not the numbers—it's the people that make up the numbers that motivate us. While we should definitely be reaching out beyond the walls of our church facilities, imagine what a difference it would make if we were just as effective welcoming those who showed up.

The first major step in the path to becoming a welcoming church is to grasp how incredibly important this ministry truly is.

MAKE THE WELCOMING CHURCH A LEADERSHIP PRIORITY

I love pastors and other church leaders. I really do.

But they are pulled in so many different directions. An overwhelming number of requests and distractions are common features of their lives every day.

So where should church leaders spend their time?

We begin with the Bible. The early church leaders, when confronted with ministries that would pull them away from their priorities, made this declaration in Acts 6:4: "But we will devote ourselves to prayer and to the ministry of the word."

That's pretty clear. The first priorities are spending time in prayer and the Word of God. Then what?

Though I would not suggest my priorities are universal for all church leaders, I do encourage them to give leadership focus to the "three Gs."

The first G is *going.* The church leader should always be prayerfully leading the church to be obedient to the Great Commission.

The second G is *groups.* The spiritually healthy church members are typically in a small group. They share the gospel more. They read the Bible more frequently. They volunteer more freely. And they give more generously.

The third G is *guests.* By this point in the book, I hope you see why and how welcoming ministries are so important. A welcoming ministry with the leadership and support of the pastor and other church leaders is a welcoming ministry likely to make a difference.

GATHER A TEAM OF PASSIONATE SERVERS

Regardless of the size of your church, you will need several people to carry out the welcoming ministry well. This team must include those with a servant's heart, those with an "other" focus.

The apostle Paul powerfully describes the role of servanthood in Philippians 2, where he wrote that becoming a servant means following the example of Christ. That example, though, is one that took Jesus to the cross.

We need welcoming team members who respond positively to the admonition of Paul in Philippians 2:3: "Do nothing out of selfish ambition or conceit, but in humility consider others more important than yourselves."

Wow! Imagine a team of committed members treating people in this manner, including church guests. It would be transformational for them and for the church.

Those servants are critical to the effectiveness of a welcoming ministry. They set an example and tone for others to follow.

CHANGE SOMETHING EVERY QUARTER

Any type of ministry or relationship can grow stale. We can get in ruts and routines. And when we get in ruts and routines, we take our relationships and ministries for granted.

I heard about this approach for the first time several years ago at a church in Arizona. The non-denominational church had done very well with its welcome ministry for two years. As a result, the number of returning guests was very high. But the ministry grew stale and routine. Enthusiasm and commitment for the welcome ministry declined.

Then the number of returning guests dropped precipitously. Guests obviously recognized intuitively that those in the welcome ministry were going through the motions more than sincerely taking the posture of a servant.

The pastor of the church recognized the pattern of routine that resulted in staleness. He began to change some parts of the welcome ministry to bring fresh ideas to it. And because the changes brought noticeable fruit, he developed his own pattern of changing something in the ministry every quarter.

For example, in one quarter he changed the way guests were welcomed in the worship services. In another quarter, he changed the specific assignments of the greeters. In the third quarter, the pastor asked every greeter to write a handwritten note to a guest on five occasions over a three-month period. Then, in the fourth quarter, they changed the welcome gifts completely.

Any relationship needs an intentional refresh on occasion. And most ministries do as well.

GIVE THE GUESTS SOMETHING TO REMEMBER THE CHURCH

A pastor in Wisconsin recounted his experience to me. "I went to the home of a family that had visited our church a few times," he told me. "It's tough to make in-home visits in our community, but they asked me to come over. It was a couple in their thirties, with three younger kids."

The pastor recounts the first thing he saw when he sat at the kitchen table. "There was a mug on the kitchen counter, " he said. "It was the mug we give to our first-time guests. Janet, the wife, noticed me looking at it. She commented that the mug was a constant reminder of their visits to our church. And she said it was a good thing."

The pastor continued, "Here is the bottom line. This couple made decisions to follow Christ. They had never been to church until they visited us. And that mug was a constant reminder for them to come back. Now I can't say they wouldn't have made the same decisions with or without a mug. But I can tell you our church won't stop giving guests gifts to remind them of us and their visits."

A small church with very limited funds refused to accept that they couldn't offer something to give to guests. So some of the ladies in the church quilted potholders with the church's initials on it. They put the potholder and a handwritten note in a small bag. Guests loved it.

As I noted earlier, I wrote the little book, *We Want You Here*, as an affordable gift to give guests. Even as I was writing it, pastors and other church leaders were telling me how they would use it in their welcome ministries.

The gift is an expression of gratitude and a reminder. And the reminder can be very important in a guest's life. For the couple in Wisconsin, the gift had an eternal connection.

UNDERSTAND THE IMPORTANCE OF LOOKING IN THE MIRROR

I provided for you an appendix for a church facility audit and a secret guest survey. Both of the resources are there to help your church evaluate itself more objectively. I call the process "looking in the mirror."

Please take the audits seriously. Have two or three people in the church do the facility audit and compare notes. See what improvements you need to make.

But have someone outside the church do the secret guest survey. Find someone who has never visited your church. Let them come in with fresh eyes. Ask them to be objective. Let them know you are not looking for all affirmations, but ways the church can really make improvements.

Conduct the guest audit once a year. Take the results of the guest audit very seriously. Read it with discernment and a listening ear. Let different leaders in the church read the results of the audit. Then prayerfully consider what changes your church can make to be a more welcoming church to those who visit you.

As an exercise of accountability and action, write a thank-you note to the guest who did the guest audit. Let him or her know what you heard, and the improvements the church plans to make. Take it seriously and respond to it prayerfully.

It is so easy to get comfortable doing church the way we've always done it. Conducting these audits is at least one way to shake us out of our complacency toward becoming that church that truly is a welcoming church.

A POSTSCRIPT OF PRIORITY

Church leaders find themselves in paradoxical times. On the one hand, there is great frustration and even futility. Churches are struggling and declining. Some are on the precipice of closing, and many more have shut their doors.

On the other hand, church leaders have so many opportunities. In almost any community, there are countless numbers of people who are not in church and have not responded to the gospel. And these unchurched people are neither resistant to the gospel nor adversarial toward the church. Indeed, many of them are seeking or waiting for an invitation from us.

The Millennials and their kids. The Millennials, born between 1980 and 2000, represent the largest generation in America's history. Over 78 million younger adults could be in our churches, but fewer than one out of five actually do attend church.

But our research indicates a growing receptivity to the gospel and church. The Millennials are hardly antagonistic. They may be more apathetic about our congregations and our message, but most of them are not resistant.

And now that many of the Millennials are parents, they are reconsidering their priorities. Their children are the next big generation. They are Generation Z or iGen or some other name that has yet to stick. These two generations represent massive waves of opportunities for our church. And they may grow more receptive to a message of hope represented by messengers of hope.

The Millennials and their kids are here. And they are coming to your church.

Cultural frustration. It hasn't been that long ago when the culture of churches and Christianity was the culture of our communities. At least on the surface, many of our values were the values of the rest of the communities around us.

No so much today.

Church leaders and church members become increasingly frustrated with the world around us. We don't understand why so many members of our communities see things so differently than we do.

So we often withdraw. We see the church as a fortress to keep us away from the pagan culture around us. We do things the way we've always done them because we find our comfort and security in them.

But we also stopped reaching people. We are more concerned about our comfort, our fortress, and our desires that we no longer are a church. Our retreat from impacting culture has turned us into a social club for religious observation.

And our churches decline. Some die.

That's what happens when we retreat. That's what happens when we are no longer a welcoming church.

But to welcome means to go as well.

Welcoming means going. Before I conclude this book, let's be clear on a major issue. The welcoming church is not merely a church that waits for the world to arrive at the physical address of the congregation. I do not want to leave with you the impression that the Great Commission is about waiting for people to come to us.

The welcoming church is more of an attitude or disposition. It represents the mind-set of an outward focus rather than an inward focus. It is about serving rather than being served.

Do you remember the story of Steve, the introvert who became the founding member of our church's welcoming ministry? Well, the rest of the story is really cool.

Steve learned to be comfortable talking to guests about the church as they arrived. He learned if he focused on others, everything else fell into place.

He took that disposition outside the walls of the church facilities. He learned to have natural and easy conversations about his faith and his Lord. A lot of people listened. A lot of people decided to follow Christ.

Steve learned that people in a welcoming church have two major dispositions. First, they look beyond themselves. They are the antithesis of those members who want everything their way: the music, the facilities, the times of services, and on and on and on. Those are the self-serving members. They see church as more like a country club where they pay their dues and get their perks and privileges.

Steve represented those church members who are other-focused. They are so busy looking to the needs of others that they don't have time to obsess over things that may not go their way. And that brings us to the second disposition.

A welcoming church is a going church. The members realize that church is not a place confined to walls, but a people determined to go. They demonstrate caring and the love of Christ in their workplaces, in their neighborhoods, in the places they shop, and in all the places where they encounter people in their communities.

Those people in the community see Christ in the welcoming church members. They decide to visit the church. And when they come to the church, they are welcomed, truly welcomed.

That's what the Great Commission is all about.

That's what welcoming churches are all about.

Is your church truly a welcoming church?

The answer to that question has eternal implications.

··· POINTS TO PONDER ···

1. Review Philippians 2:3. Relate the details of that verse to becoming a welcoming church.
2. What qualifications should a member of a church welcoming ministry have?
3. Explain the importance and significance of a secret guest survey. Who should do the secret guest survey for your church? How often should you conduct the survey?
4. What can your church do more effectively to reach the Millennial generation and their children?
5. Why must a welcoming church also be a going church?

OTHER RESOURCES BY THOM S. RAINER

Blog

www.ThomRainer.com

Podcasts

Rainer on Leadership

Revitalize and Replant

Subscription Ministry

Church Answers

CHURCH FACILITY AUDIT

This audit should be completed by at least five church members. Each member should select a different time to view the church. This particular survey should be done during the week, and not during weekend services.

For each item, you will provide a score from 1 to 10. The lowest score means "totally inadequate," and the highest score means "nearly perfect."

Try to imagine you have never seen your church facilities or website. Do your best to form a "first impression."

After all the members have completed the surveys, they should meet with key leaders in the church to discuss their findings. From there, a task force can be formed to improve overall guest friendliness on the website and in the facilities.

CIRCLE ONE NUMBER FOR EACH AREA.

CHURCH WEBSITE

Is it attractive? Functional? Free of errors? Up to date? Are the times of services and address listed?

TOTALLY INADEQUATE // MARGINALLY ACCEPTABLE // ACCEPTABLE // NEARLY PERFECT

1 2 3 4 5 6 7 8 9 10

EXTERIOR SIGNAGE

Visible from street? Worship center clearly marked? Office entrance clearly marked?

TOTALLY INADEQUATE // MARGINALLY ACCEPTABLE // ACCEPTABLE // NEARLY PERFECT

1 2 3 4 5 6 7 8 9 10

PARKING LOT

Clear signage direction? Neat appearance? Handicap parking? Guest parking? Other?

TOTALLY INADEQUATE // MARGINALLY ACCEPTABLE // ACCEPTABLE // NEARLY PERFECT

1 2 3 4 5 6 7 8 9 10

GENERAL EXTERIOR APPEARANCE

Neat exterior of building? Well landscaped? Pleasing to the sight? Kept up well?

TOTALLY INADEQUATE // MARGINALLY ACCEPTABLE // ACCEPTABLE // NEARLY PERFECT

1 2 3 4 5 6 7 8 9 10

INTERIOR SIGNAGE

Clear directions to offices, worship center, preschool, welcome center, etc?

TOTALLY INADEQUATE // MARGINALLY ACCEPTABLE // ACCEPTABLE // NEARLY PERFECT

1 2 3 4 5 6 7 8 9 10

GENERAL INTERIOR APPEARANCE

Neat? Up to date? Furniture? Lack of "junk" lying around? Well cared for? Clean? Adedequate number of trash cans? Neat and clean interior paint?

TOTALLY INADEQUATE // MARGINALLY ACCEPTABLE // ACCEPTABLE // NEARLY PERFECT

1 2 3 4 5 6 7 8 9 10

WORSHIP CENTER/SANCTUARY

Pleasing to the eye? Well kept furniture? Lack of "junk" lying around? Well cared for? Clean? Interior paint? Neat hymnals, Bibles, guest cards, pens, etc?

TOTALLY INADEQUATE // MARGINALLY ACCEPTABLE // ACCEPTABLE // NEARLY PERFECT

1 2 3 4 5 6 7 8 9 10

RESTROOMS

Good locations? Adequate number? Adequate numbers of toilets? Clean? Well supplied? Up to date? Clean and adequate soap and hand dryers?

TOTALLY INADEQUATE // MARGINALLY ACCEPTABLE // ACCEPTABLE // NEARLY PERFECT

1 2 3 4 5 6 7 8 9 10

CHILDREN'S AREAS/PRESCHOOL/NURSERY

Clean? Modern furniture? Newer toys? Appearance of security? Overall sense of security for safety and sanitation if you left your own child or grandchild there?

TOTALLY INADEQUATE // MARGINALLY ACCEPTABLE // ACCEPTABLE // NEARLY PERFECT

1 2 3 4 5 6 7 8 9 10

OVERALL APPEARANCE OF CHURCH FACILITIES

Compared to other churches? Compared to secular organizations? Cleanliness? Up to date? Space? Hallways? Foyers?

TOTALLY INADEQUATE // MARGINALLY ACCEPTABLE // ACCEPTABLE // NEARLY PERFECT

1 2 3 4 5 6 7 8 9 10

NOW ADD ALL THE NUMBERS YOU CIRCLED AND PUT YOUR TOTAL HERE: ____

10 – 39. VERY BAD. YOUR CHURCH IS IN VERY BAD CONDITION WITH ITS WEBSITE AND FACILITIES. IMMEDIATE AND REMEDIAL ACTIONS ARE NEEDED.

40 – 69. BARELY ACCEPTABLE. THOUGH YOUR CHURCH FACILITY AND WEBSITE HAVE SOME STRENGTHS, THERE ARE STILL SEVERAL REMEDIAL ACTIONS THAT SHOULD BE MADE OVER THE NEXT SIX MONTHS.

70 – 89. ACCEPTABLE TO ABOVE AVERAGE. YOUR CHURCH WEBSITE AND FACILITY ARE BETTER THAN MOST OTHER CHURCHES. SOME TWEAKS COULD BE MADE TO MAKE IT EVEN BETTER.

90 – 100. INCREDIBLE. YOUR CHURCH WEBSITE AND FACILITY ARE AMONG THE BEST IN THE NATION. KEEP UP THE GOOD WORK.

SECRET GUEST SURVEY

CHURCH NAME

Thank you for taking time to be a secret church guest at our church. You are truly providing a helpful ministry to us. While we do not expect you to answer all of these questions in your report, we provide them as a general guide for you in this process.

If you do not have sufficient space, please add space electronically, or add pages if you are completing this report manually. If you have questions after reviewing this document, feel free to contact us at

A. Prior to going to the church, review the means to determine the location of the church and times for the church services:

1. Does the church have a website? If so, is it helpful? User-friendly? Does it provide the information you need to get to the church on time?

2. What conclusions do you reach about the church based on its website?

B. Having driven to the church and entered the parking lot, consider these questions:

1. Was it difficult to find the building? Would a person naturally drive by this building, or must you be intentionally going to this building to find it?

2. What are your thoughts as you view this church from the road? Based upon your first view of the buildings, what is your impression of the church?

3. Is there a church sign? If so, is it helpful?

4. Is guest parking available? If so, how is it marked? Are there signs directing you to guest parking?

5. Are there greeters in the parking lot?

6. Is the parking lot adequate? Convenient to the main entrance?

7. Is there a convenient auto passenger loading/unloading area? Is it covered for use in inclement weather?

8. Is it easy to locate the main entrance? Do you immediately know where to go to enter for church services?

C. As you enter the church, consider these questions:

1. As you enter, what are your first impressions of the entry foyer?

   Rate the following characteristics on a scale of 1 to 5:

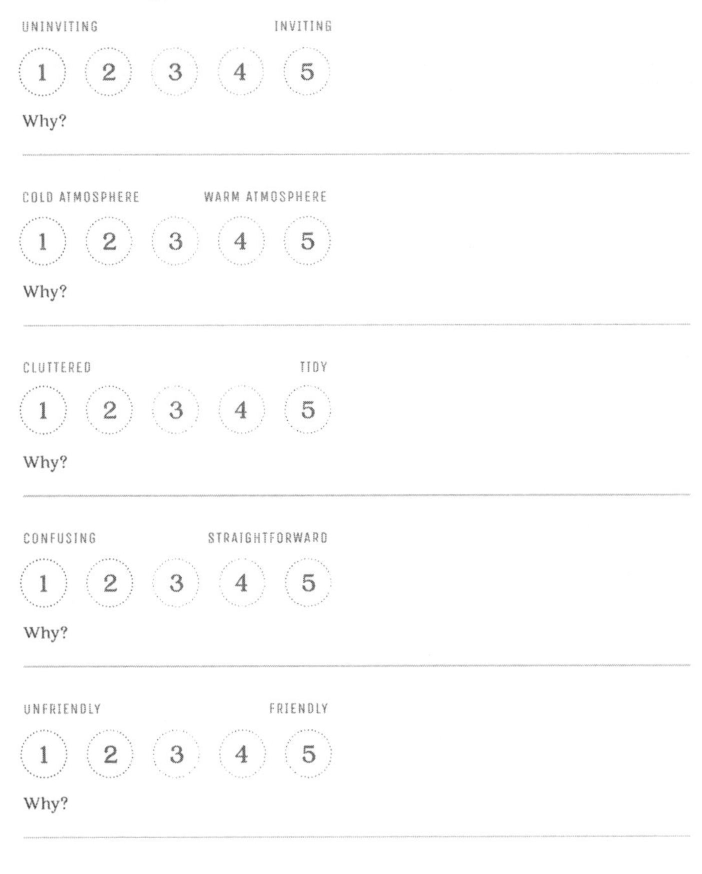

UNINVITING — INVITING

1 2 3 4 5

Why?

COLD ATMOSPHERE — WARM ATMOSPHERE

1 2 3 4 5

Why?

CLUTTERED — TIDY

1 2 3 4 5

Why?

CONFUSING — STRAIGHTFORWARD

1 2 3 4 5

Why?

UNFRIENDLY — FRIENDLY

1 2 3 4 5

Why?

2. Is there adequate space in the foyer for people to talk and fellowship before and after worship services without blocking the main circulation path?

3. Is the circulation pattern clear?
   Do you know how to get to various areas of the building?

4. Is there a clearly marked guest/welcome center?

5. Are there adequate signs to help you find your way?

D. If you attend a small group (which is strongly our preference), respond to these questions:

1. Are there greeters who help you get to the appropriate classroom?

2. What is your first reaction to the education areas?

3. Do the classrooms appear large enough to make them usable for various age groups and teaching methods?

4. Are there room identification signs?

5. If you have children, is there a security/identification process in place to help identify your child/children?

6. How do you feel about leaving your children in the classrooms?
(IMPORTANT: IF YOU HAVE ANY DISCOMFORT AT ALL, DO NOT LEAVE YOUR CHILDREN).

7. Do the classroom leaders secure needed information from you (e.g., name, address, allergies for children, your location in the building if needed in an emergency)?

8. Do preschool and children's rooms communicate a sense of security and warmth?

9. After attending a small group, rate the experience on the basis of:
   a. quality of the teaching

   b. friendliness of the group

   c. preparedness of the group – that is, were they ready to welcome and include a guest?

10. Would you attend a small group at this church again?

E. In the worship center, consider these questions:

1. What are your first feelings and thoughts as you enter? Why?

2. Does this space feel welcoming? Why?

3. Does the worship space say anything to you about this congregation and its priorities?

4. Is there appropriate quality in materials and craftsmanship? Does anything look cheap, too showy, out of place?

E. In the worship center, consider these questions:

1. What are your first feelings and thoughts as you enter? Why?

2. Does this space feel welcoming? Why?

3. Does the worship space say anything to you about this congregation and its priorities?

4. Is there appropriate quality in materials and craftsmanship? Does anything look cheap, too showy, out of place?

6. As a guest, did you feel uncomfortable in any way? Affirmed in any way?

7. If the church provided you any documents (e.g., bulletin, worship guide, etc.), are the documents high quality? Did they facilitate worship for you in any way?

8. Rate the overall experience on the basis of:
   a. quality of the music

   b. style of the music

   c. friendliness of the congregation

   d. quality of the preaching

   e. clarity in instruction – did you know and understand what the church expected participants to do at all points in the service?

   f. use of PowerPoint or other media to make announcements, outline sermon, etc.

9. What one improvement would you suggest regarding the worship service?

10. Would you return to this church to worship with this congregation?

F. Summary

1. What are your overall impressions of this church based on this visit?

2. Would you return to visit this church? Why or why not?

Your goal is to provide us information that simply tells your experience in this church.
Be honest and clear.
Thank you again for your willingness to assist

CHURCH NAME

ALSO AVAILABLE
A GIFT FOR YOUR CHURCH GUEST

The message is basic yet profound.
This book is a gift for guests and communicates
that they are welcome in your church.

$12.99, 978-1-4627-8089-1

Churches can buy in bulk for $5/book in box of 20 ($100 total).